MW00883523

THIS JOURNAL BELONGS TO:

_____

_____

_____

"If you want something you've never had, you must be willing to do something you've never done."

— *Thomas Jefferson, Third President of the United States*

INDEX:

MY BODY EVALUATION

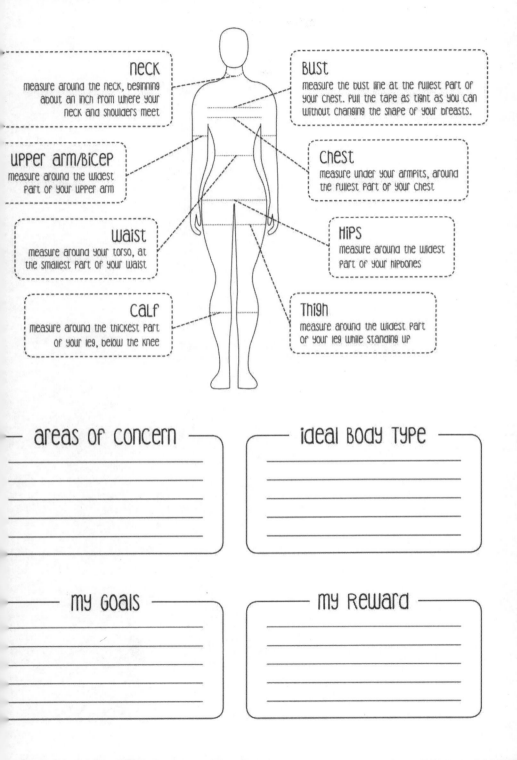

neck
measure around the neck, beginning about an inch from where your neck and shoulders meet

Bust
measure the bust line at the fullest part of your chest. Pull the tape as tight as you can without changing the shape of your breasts.

upper arm/Bicep
measure around the widest part of your upper arm

Chest
measure under your armpits, around the fullest part of your chest

waist
measure around your torso, at the smallest part of your waist

Hips
measure around the widest part of your hipbones

Calf
measure around the thickest part of your leg, below the knee

Thigh
measure around the widest part of your leg while standing up

— areas of concern —

— ideal BODY TYPE —

— my Goals —

— my Reward —

BEFORE & AFTER

The OLD me

```
PLACE YOUR PICTURE
HERE

2.25" X 3"
5cm X 7.50cm
```

The new me

```
PLACE YOUR PICTURE
HERE

2.25" X 3"
5cm X 7.50cm
```

Before	Stats & Measurements	After
	Weight	
	BMI	
	Body Fat Percentage	
	Muscle Percentage	
	Neck	
	Bust/Chest	
	Upper Arm/Bicep	
	Waist	
	Hips	
	Thigh	
	Calf	

WEIGHT LOSS TRACKER

⊡ Track your weight ⊡

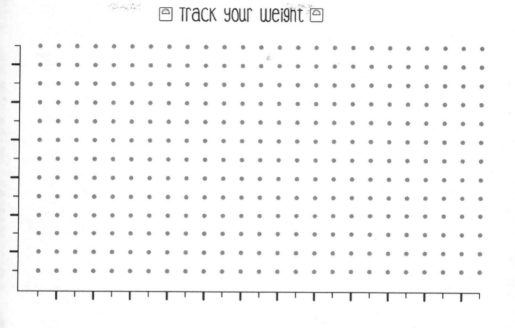

⊡ Track your measurements ⊡

Date										
y fat %										
neck										
st/chest										
Biceps										
waist										
Hips										
Thigh										
calf										

mon	tue	wed	thur	fri	sat	sun

my goals this month

monthly stats

workout	rest days

what worked

what didn't work

30 DAY AB CHALLENGE

crunches

5	10	15	20	25	Rest	30	35
40	45	50	Rest	55	60	65	70
75	Rest	80	85	90	95	100	Rest
105	110	115	120	125			

Plank

sec	5 sec	10 sec	10 sec	Rest	15 sec	15 sec	20 sec
sec	Rest	25 sec	25 sec	30 sec	30 sec	Rest	35 sec
sec	40 sec	40 sec	Rest	45 sec	45 sec	50 sec	50 sec
est	55 sec	55 sec	60 sec	60 sec			

Sit-ups

5	10	15	20	25	Rest	30	35
40	45	50	Rest	55	60	65	70
75	Rest	80	85	90	95	100	Rest
05	110	115	120	125			

Leg Raises

0	13	16	19	22	Rest	25	28
31	34	37	Rest	40	43	46	49
52	Rest	55	58	61	64	67	Rest
0	73	76	79	82			

30 DAY FITNESS CHALLENGE

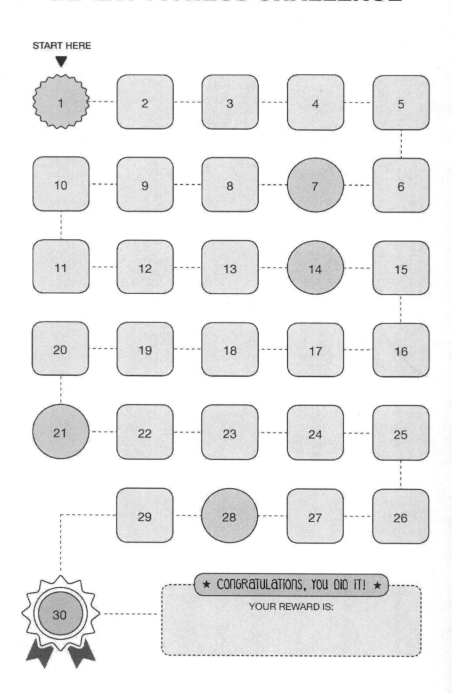

START HERE

★ CONGRATULATIONS, YOU DID IT! ★

YOUR REWARD IS:

WEEK 1

"No pain, no gain. Shut up and train."

Priorities

- _____
- _____
- _____
- _____
- _____
- _____
- _____
- _____
- _____
- _____

My Goals

My Motivation

measurements

neck _____
chest _____
biceps _____
waist _____
hips _____
thigh _____
calf _____

weight

weight _____
bmi _____
fat% _____

WEEK 2

"Train insane or remain the same."

m
🌢🌢🌢🌢🌢🌢🌢🌢 😣 🙂 😐 😟 😫

T
🌢🌢🌢🌢🌢🌢🌢🌢 😣 🙂 😐 😟 😫

W
🌢🌢🌢🌢🌢🌢🌢🌢 😣 🙂 😐 😟 😫

T
🌢🌢🌢🌢🌢🌢🌢🌢 😣 🙂 😐 😟 😫

f
🌢🌢🌢🌢🌢🌢🌢🌢 😣 🙂 😐 😟 😫

S
🌢🌢🌢🌢🌢🌢🌢🌢 😣 🙂 😐 😟 😫

S
🌢🌢🌢🌢🌢🌢🌢🌢 😣 🙂 😐 😟 😫

⇶⟶ Priorities ⟵⇇

- ☐ _____
- ☐ _____
- ☐ _____
- ☐ _____
- ☐ _____
- ☐ _____
- ☐ _____
- ☐ _____
- ☐ _____

my Goals

my motivation

⊬ measurements ⊬

neck _____
chest _____
Biceps _____
waist _____
Hips _____
Thigh _____
calf _____

🚹 weight 🚹

weight _____
BMi _____
fat% _____

"Push yourself because no one else is going to do it for you."

Priorities

- [ ] _____
- [ ] _____
- [ ] _____
- [ ] _____
- [ ] _____
- [ ] _____
- [ ] _____
- [ ] _____
- [ ] _____
- [ ] _____
- [ ] _____

My Goals

My Motivation

Measurements

neck _____
chest _____
biceps _____
waist _____
hips _____
thigh _____
calf _____

Weight

weight _____
BMI _____
fat% _____

WEEK 4

"Suck it up. And one day you won't have to suck it in."

m

T

W

T

f

S

S

⟫⟶⟶ Priorities ⟵⟵

- _____
- _____
- _____
- _____
- _____
- _____
- _____
- _____
- _____
- _____

--- my Goals ---

--- my motivation

🦌 measurements 🦌

neck _____
chest _____
Biceps _____
waist _____
Hips _____
Thigh _____
calf _____

🏋 weight 🏋 —

weight _____
BMi _____
fat% _____

WEIGHT LOSS TRACKER

 Track your weight

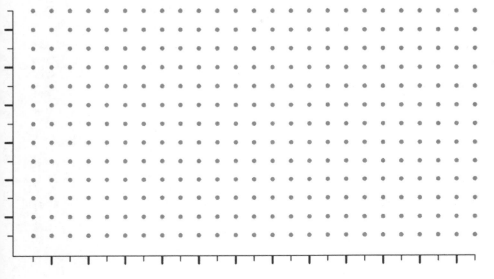

Track your measurements

Date										
y fat %										
neck										
t/chest										
Biceps										
Waist										
Hips										
Thigh										
Calf										

my goals this month

monthly stats

workout	Rest Days

what worked

what didn't work

mon	Tue	wed	Thur	fri	Sat	Sun

30 DAY ARM CHALLENGE

PUSH-UPS

5	5	10	10	Rest	15	15	20
20	Rest	25	25	30	30	Rest	35
35	40	40	Rest	45	45	50	50
Rest	55	55	60	60			

BICEP CURLS

5	10	15	20	25	Rest	30	35
40	45	50	Rest	55	60	65	70
75	Rest	80	85	90	95	100	Rest
105	110	115	120	125			

PUNCHES

sec	5 sec	10 sec	10 sec	Rest	15 sec	15 sec	20 sec
sec	Rest	25 sec	25 sec	30 sec	30 sec	Rest	35 sec
sec	40 sec	40 sec	Rest	45 sec	45 sec	50 sec	50 sec
est	55 sec	55 sec	60 sec	60 sec			

MOUNTAIN CLIMBERS

5	10	15	20	25	Rest	30	35
40	45	50	Rest	55	60	65	70
75	Rest	80	85	90	95	100	Rest
105	110	115	120	125			

30 DAY FITNESS CHALLENGE

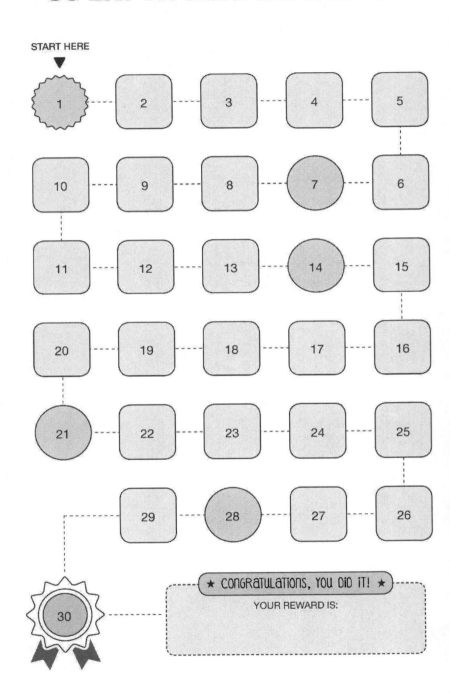

START HERE

1 --- 2 --- 3 --- 4 --- 5

10 --- 9 --- 8 --- 7 --- 6

11 --- 12 --- 13 --- 14 --- 15

20 --- 19 --- 18 --- 17 --- 16

21 --- 22 --- 23 --- 24 --- 25

29 --- 28 --- 27 --- 26

30

★ CONGRATULATIONS, YOU DID IT! ★

YOUR REWARD IS:

WEEK 5

"Success starts with self-discipline."

Priorities

- _____
- _____
- _____
- _____
- _____
- _____
- _____
- _____
- _____
- _____

my goals

my motivation

measurements

neck _____
chest _____
biceps _____
waist _____
hips _____
thigh _____
calf _____

weight

weight _____
bmi _____
fat% _____

WEEK 6

"Good things come to those who sweat."

m

T

W

T

f

S

S

- _____
- _____
- _____
- _____
- _____
- _____
- _____
- _____
- _____

--- my Goals ---

--- my motivation ---

🦌 measurements 🦌

neck _____
chest _____
biceps _____
waist _____
hips _____
thigh _____
calf _____

— ⚖ weight ⚖ —

weight _____
bmi _____
fat% _____

"Motivation is what gets you started. Habit is what keeps you going."

⇢ Priorities ⇠

○ _____
○ _____
○ _____
○ _____
○ _____
○ _____
○ _____
○ _____
○ _____
○ _____

My Goals

My Motivation

🖐 measurements 🖐

Neck _____
Chest _____
Biceps _____
Waist _____
Hips _____
Thigh _____
Calf _____

🧍 Weight 🧍

Weight _____
BMI _____
Fat% _____

WEEK 8

"A one hour workout is 4% of your day. No excuses.

m

◊ ◊ ◊ ◊ ◊ ◊ ◊ ◊ 😋 🙂 😐 🙁 😫

T

◊ ◊ ◊ ◊ ◊ ◊ ◊ ◊ 😋 🙂 😐 🙁 😫

W

◊ ◊ ◊ ◊ ◊ ◊ ◊ ◊ 😋 🙂 😐 🙁 😫

T

◊ ◊ ◊ ◊ ◊ ◊ ◊ ◊ 😋 🙂 😐 🙁 😫

f

◊ ◊ ◊ ◊ ◊ ◊ ◊ ◊ 😋 🙂 😐 🙁 😫

S

◊ ◊ ◊ ◊ ◊ ◊ ◊ ◊ 😋 🙂 😐 🙁 😫

S

◊ ◊ ◊ ◊ ◊ ◊ ◊ ◊ 😋 🙂 😐 🙁 😫

≫→ Priorities ←≪

- ◌ _____
- ◌ _____
- ◌ _____
- ◌ _____
- ◌ _____
- ◌ _____
- ◌ _____
- ◌ _____
- ◌ _____
- ◌ _____

my Goals

my motivation

measurements

neck _____
chest _____
Biceps _____
waist _____
Hips _____
Thigh _____
calf _____

weight

weight _____
BMi _____
fat% _____

WEIGHT LOSS TRACKER

Track your weight

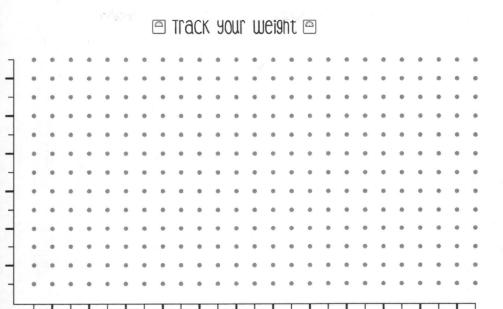

Track your measurements

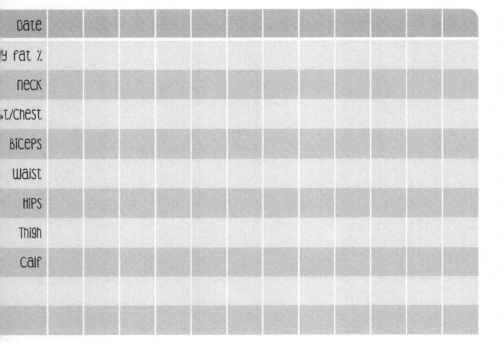

Date								
y fat %								
neck								
t/chest								
Biceps								
Waist								
Hips								
Thigh								
Calf								

mon	Tue	Wed	Thur	Fri	Sat	Sun

my goals this month

monthly stats

workout	
Rest Days	

what worked

what didn't work

30 DAY GLUTE CHALLENGE

Lunges (each Leg)

5	10	15	20	25	Rest	30	35
40	45	50	Rest	55	60	65	70
75	Rest	80	85	90	95	100	Rest
105	110	115	120	125			

Squats

5	10	15	20	25	Rest	30	35
40	45	50	Rest	55	60	65	70
75	Rest	80	85	90	95	100	Rest
105	110	115	120	125			

Pulse Squats

5	5	10	10	Rest	15	15	20
20	Rest	25	25	30	30	Rest	35
35	40	40	Rest	45	45	50	50
Rest	55	55	60	60			

Fire Hydrants (each Leg)

10	13	16	19	22	Rest	25	28
31	34	37	Rest	40	43	46	49
52	Rest	55	58	61	64	67	Rest
70	73	76	79	82			

30 DAY FITNESS CHALLENGE

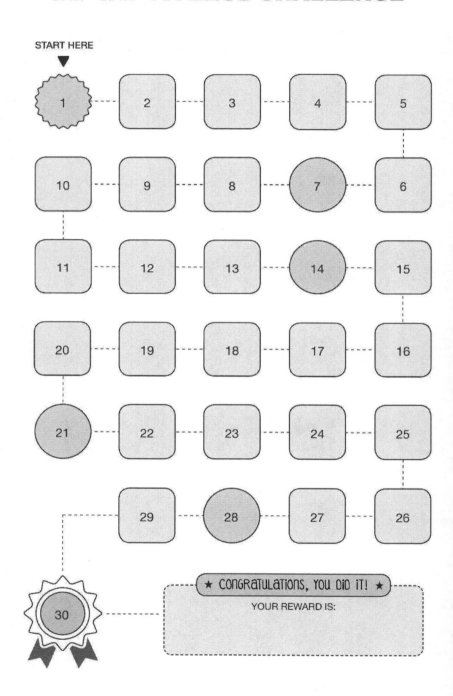

START HERE

1   2   3   4   5

10   9   8   7   6

11   12   13   14   15

20   19   18   17   16

21   22   23   24   25

29   28   27   26

30

★ Congratulations, you did it! ★

YOUR REWARD IS:

WEEK 9

"The body achieves what the mind believes."

○○○○○○○○ 😊 🙂 😐 😟 😣

○○○○○○○○ 😊 🙂 😐 😟 😣

○○○○○○○○ 😊 🙂 😐 😟 😣

○○○○○○○○ 😊 🙂 😐 😟 😣

○○○○○○○○ 😊 🙂 😐 😟 😣

○○○○○○○○ 😊 🙂 😐 😟 😣

○○○○○○○○ 😊 🙂 😐 😟 😣

≫→ Priorities ←≪

- _____
- _____
- _____
- _____
- _____
- _____
- _____
- _____
- _____
- _____

my Goals

my motivation

measurements

neck _____
chest _____
biceps _____
waist _____
hips _____
thigh _____
calf _____

weight

weight _____
BMi _____
fat% _____

WEEK 10

"What seems impossible today will one day become your warm-up"

m

T

W

T

f

S

S

➤➤➤ Priorities ⟵⟵

○ _____
○ _____
○ _____
○ _____
○ _____
○ _____
○ _____
○ _____
○ _____
○ _____

--- my Goals ---

--- my motivation

🦌 measurements

neck _____
chest _____
biceps _____
waist _____
hips _____
thigh _____
calf _____

— 🔒 weight 🔒 —

weight _____
BMi _____
fat% _____

"Someone busier than you is working out right now."

- ☐ _____
- ☐ _____
- ☐ _____
- ☐ _____
- ☐ _____
- ☐ _____
- ☐ _____
- ☐ _____
- ☐ _____
- ☐ _____

My Goals

My Motivation

measurements

neck _____
chest _____
biceps _____
waist _____
hips _____
thigh _____
calf _____

weight

weight _____
bmi _____
fat% _____

WEEK 12

"Hustle for that muscle."

m

T

W

T

f

S

S

- _____
- _____
- _____
- _____
- _____
- _____
- _____
- _____
- _____
- _____

------ my Goals ------

------ my motivation

🐐 measurements

neck _____
chest _____
biceps _____
waist _____
Hips _____
Thigh _____
calf _____

—— ⚖ weight ⚖ ——

weight _____
BMi _____
fat% _____

WEIGHT LOSS TRACKER

Track your weight

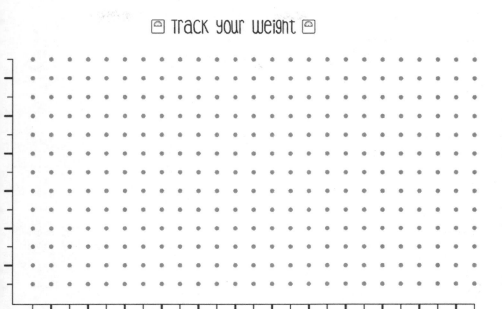

Track your measurements

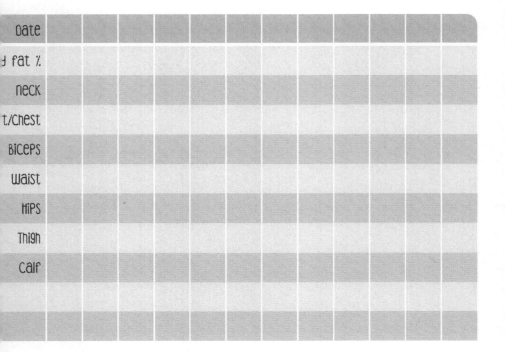

Date										
fat %										
neck										
t/chest										
Biceps										
Waist										
Hips										
Thigh										
Calf										

mon	tue	wed	thur	fri	sat	sun

my goals this month

monthly stats

workout	rest days

what worked

what didn't work

30 DAY AB CHALLENGE

Crunches

5	10	15	20	25	Rest	30	35
40	45	50	Rest	55	60	65	70
75	Rest	80	85	90	95	100	Rest
105	110	115	120	125			

Plank

sec	5 sec	10 sec	10 sec	Rest	15 sec	15 sec	20 sec
sec	Rest	25 sec	25 sec	30 sec	30 sec	Rest	35 sec
sec	40 sec	40 sec	Rest	45 sec	45 sec	50 sec	50 sec
Rest	55 sec	55 sec	60 sec	60 sec			

Sit-ups

5	10	15	20	25	Rest	30	35
40	45	50	Rest	55	60	65	70
75	Rest	80	85	90	95	100	Rest
05	110	115	120	125			

Leg Raises

10	13	16	19	22	Rest	25	28
31	34	37	Rest	40	43	46	49
52	Rest	55	58	61	64	67	Rest
70	73	76	79	82			

30 DAY FITNESS CHALLENGE

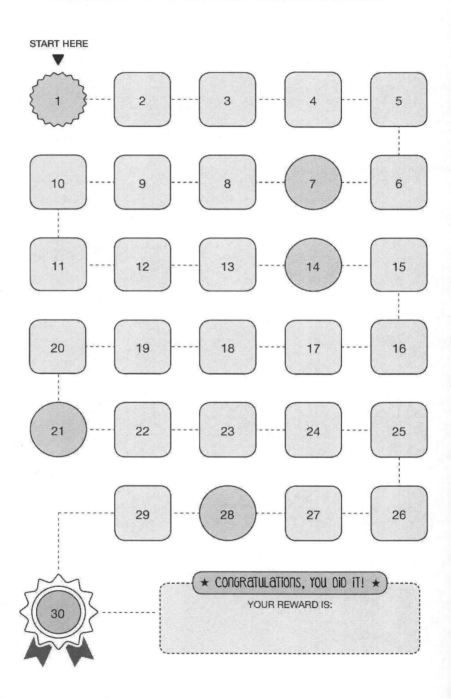

START HERE

1 2 3 4 5

10 9 8 7 6

11 12 13 14 15

20 19 18 17 16

21 22 23 24 25

29 28 27 26

30

★ CONGRATULATIONS, YOU DID IT! ★

YOUR REWARD IS:

"Work hard in silence. Let success be your noise."

ⴋⴋⴋⴋⴋⴋⴋⴋ 😃 🙂 😐 🙁 😣

ⴋⴋⴋⴋⴋⴋⴋⴋ 😃 🙂 😐 🙁 😣

ⴋⴋⴋⴋⴋⴋⴋⴋ 😃 🙂 😐 🙁 😣

ⴋⴋⴋⴋⴋⴋⴋⴋ 😃 🙂 😐 🙁 😣

ⴋⴋⴋⴋⴋⴋⴋⴋ 😃 🙂 😐 🙁 😣

ⴋⴋⴋⴋⴋⴋⴋⴋ 😃 🙂 😐 🙁 😣

ⴋⴋⴋⴋⴋⴋⴋⴋ 😃 🙂 😐 🙁 😣

Priorities

- _____
- _____
- _____
- _____
- _____
- _____
- _____
- _____
- _____
- _____

My Goals

My Motivation

Measurements

Neck _____
Chest _____
Biceps _____
Waist _____
Hips _____
Thigh _____
Calf _____

Weight

Weight _____
BMI _____
Fat% _____

WEEK 14

"The hardest lift of all is lifting your butt off the couch."

m

T

W

T

f

S

S

>>→> priorities <←←

- _____
- _____
- _____
- _____
- _____
- _____
- _____
- _____
- _____

my goals

my motivation

measurements

neck _____
chest _____
biceps _____
waist _____
hips _____
thigh _____
calf _____

weight

weight _____
BMI _____
fat% _____

WEEK 15

"When you feel like quitting think about why you started."

⟫⟶⟩ Priorities ⟨⟵⟪

- _____
- _____
- _____
- _____
- _____
- _____
- _____
- _____
- _____
- _____

My Goals

My Motivation

👿 Measurements 👿

neck _____
chest _____
biceps _____
waist _____
hips _____
thigh _____
calf _____

🔒 Weight 🔒

weight _____
BMI _____
fat% _____

WEEK 16

"It comes down to one simple thing: how bad do you want it?"

m

🌢🌢🌢🌢🌢🌢🌢🌢 😊 😊 😐 😟 😖

T

🌢🌢🌢🌢🌢🌢🌢🌢 😊 😊 😐 😟 😖

W

🌢🌢🌢🌢🌢🌢🌢🌢 😊 😊 😐 😟 😖

T

🌢🌢🌢🌢🌢🌢🌢🌢 😊 😊 😐 😟 😖

f

🌢🌢🌢🌢🌢🌢🌢🌢 😊 😊 😐 😟 😖

S

🌢🌢🌢🌢🌢🌢🌢🌢 😊 😊 😐 😟 😖

S

🌢🌢🌢🌢🌢🌢🌢🌢 😊 😊 😐 😟 😖

⟫⟩⟩ Priorities ⟨⟨

- ☐ _____
- ☐ _____
- ☐ _____
- ☐ _____
- ☐ _____
- ☐ _____
- ☐ _____
- ☐ _____
- ☐ _____
- ☐ _____

my Goals

my motivation

🦌 measurements 🦌

neck _____
chest _____
biceps _____
waist _____
hips _____
thigh _____
calf _____

🔧 weight 🔧

weight _____
BMI _____
fat% _____

WEIGHT LOSS TRACKER

⊡ Track your weight ⊡

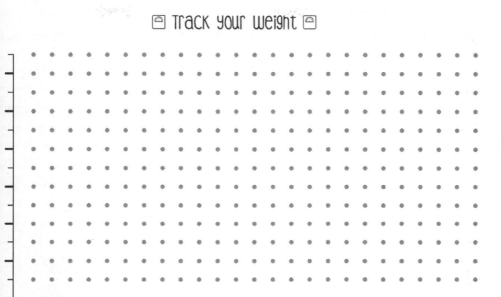

Track your measurements

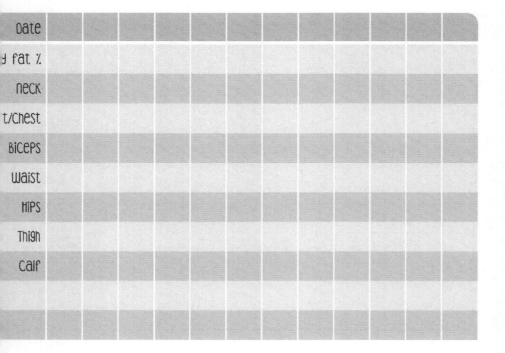

Date										
y fat %										
neck										
t/chest										
Biceps										
waist										
Hips										
Thigh										
calf										

WEEK 17

"Making excuses burns zero calories per hour."

m

T

W

T

f

S

S

Priorities

- _____
- _____
- _____
- _____
- _____
- _____
- _____
- _____
- _____
- _____

--- my Goals ---

--- my motivation

🦌 measurements 🦌

neck _____
chest _____
biceps _____
waist _____
hips _____
thigh _____
calf _____

— 🔋 weight 🔋 —

weight _____
bmi _____
fat% _____

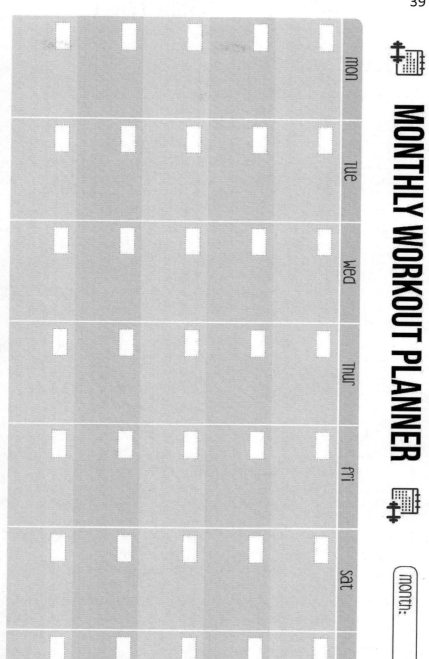

MONTHLY WORKOUT PLANNER

month:

mon	tue	wed	Thur	fri	sat	sun

my goals this month

monthly stats
Workout
Rest Days

what worked

what didn't work

30 DAY ARM CHALLENGE

PUSH-UPS

5	5	10	10	Rest	15	15	20
20	Rest	25	25	30	30	Rest	35
35	40	40	Rest	45	45	50	50
Rest	55	55	60	60			

BICEP CURLS

5	10	15	20	25	Rest	30	35
40	45	50	Rest	55	60	65	70
75	Rest	80	85	90	95	100	Re
105	110	115	120	125			

PUNCHES

5 sec	5 sec	10 sec	10 sec	Rest	15 sec	15 sec	20 s
20 sec	Rest	25 sec	25 sec	30 sec	30 sec	Rest	35 s
35 sec	40 sec	40 sec	Rest	45 sec	45 sec	50 sec	50 s
Rest	55 sec	55 sec	60 sec	60 sec			

MOUNTAIN CLIMBERS

5	10	15	20	25	Rest	30	35
40	45	50	Rest	55	60	65	70
75	Rest	80	85	90	95	100	Re
105	110	115	120	125			

30 DAY FITNESS CHALLENGE

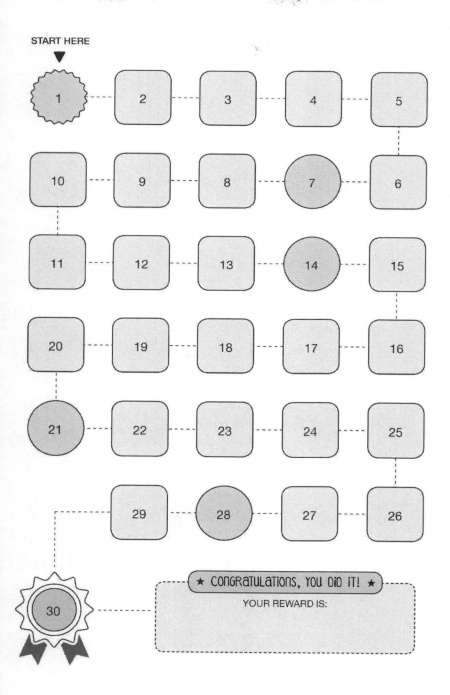

WEEK 18

"The only bad workout is the one that didn't happen."

m ○○○○○○○○○ 😔 🙂 😐 🙁 😣

T ○○○○○○○○○ 😔 🙂 😐 🙁 😣

W ○○○○○○○○○ 😔 🙂 😐 🙁 😣

T ○○○○○○○○○ 😔 🙂 😐 🙁 😣

f ○○○○○○○○○ 😔 🙂 😐 🙁 😣

S ○○○○○○○○○ 😔 🙂 😐 🙁 😣

S ○○○○○○○○○ 😔 🙂 😐 🙁 😣

Priorities

- _____
- _____
- _____
- _____
- _____
- _____
- _____
- _____
- _____

my Goals

my motivation

measurements

neck _____
chest _____
Biceps _____
waist _____
Hips _____
Thigh _____
calf _____

weight

weight _____
BMI _____
fat% _____

"The pain you feel today, will be the strength you feel tomorrow."

Priorities

- _____
- _____
- _____
- _____
- _____
- _____
- _____
- _____
- _____
- _____

my Goals

my motivation

measurements

neck _____
chest _____
Biceps _____
waist _____
Hips _____
Thigh _____
Calf _____

weight

weight _____
BMI _____
fat% _____

WEEK 20

"Don't limit your challenges, challenge your limits."

m

T

W

T

f

S

S

⋙→→ Priorities ⟵←

- _____
- _____
- _____
- _____
- _____
- _____
- _____
- _____
- _____
- _____

--- my Goals ---

--- my motivation

⚘ measurements ⚘

neck _____
chest _____
Biceps _____
waist _____
Hips _____
Thigh _____
calf _____

🏋 weight 🏋

weight _____
BMi _____
fat% _____

WEIGHT LOSS TRACKER

Track your weight

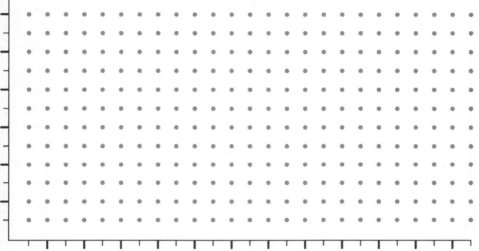

Track your measurements

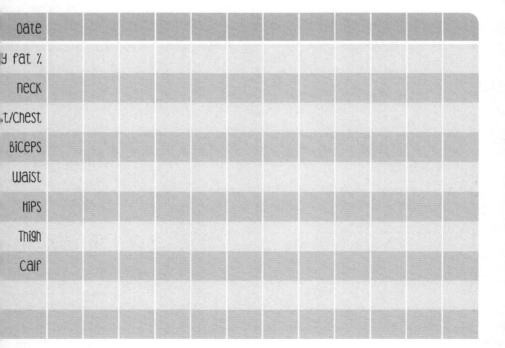

Date										
y fat %										
neck										
t/chest										
Biceps										
waist										
Hips										
Thigh										
Calf										

WEEK 21

"It's actually pretty simple. Either you do it, or you don't."

m

T

W

T

f

S

S

- _____
- _____
- _____
- _____
- _____
- _____
- _____
- _____
- _____
- _____

---- my Goals ----

---- my motivation ----

measurements

neck _____
chest _____
Biceps _____
waist _____
Hips _____
Thigh _____
Calf _____

weight

weight _____
BMi _____
fat% _____

MONTHLY WORKOUT PLANNER

month:

mon	tue	wed	Thur	fri	sat	sun

my goals this month

monthly stats
workout
Rest Days

what worked

what Didn't work

Lunges (each Leg)

5	10	15	20	25	Rest	30	35
40	45	50	Rest	55	60	65	70
75	Rest	80	85	90	95	100	Res
105	110	115	120	125			

Squats

5	10	15	20	25	Rest	30	35
40	45	50	Rest	55	60	65	70
75	Rest	80	85	90	95	100	Res
105	110	115	120	125			

Pulse Squats

5	5	10	10	Rest	15	15	20
20	Rest	25	25	30	30	Rest	35
35	40	40	Rest	45	45	50	50
Rest	55	55	60	60			

Fire Hydrants (each Leg)

10	13	16	19	22	Rest	25	28
31	34	37	Rest	40	43	46	49
52	Rest	55	58	61	64	67	Res
70	73	76	79	82			

30 DAY FITNESS CHALLENGE

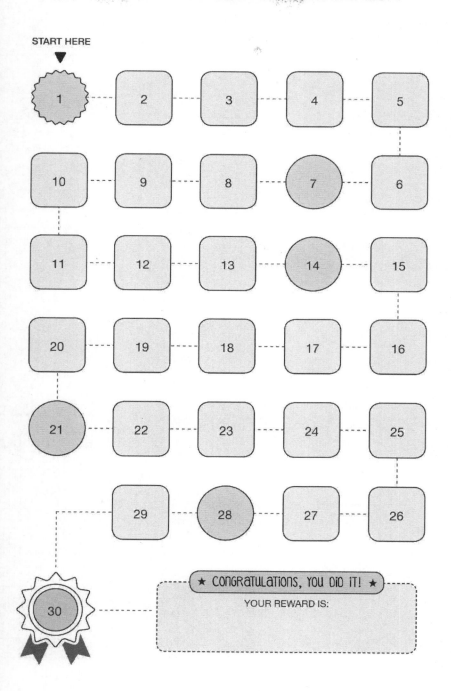

START HERE

1 — 2 — 3 — 4 — 5

10 — 9 — 8 — 7 — 6

11 — 12 — 13 — 14 — 15

20 — 19 — 18 — 17 — 16

21 — 22 — 23 — 24 — 25

29 — 28 — 27 — 26

30

★ CONGRATULATIONS, YOU DID IT! ★

YOUR REWARD IS:

WEEK 22

"Nothing truly great ever came from a comfort zone."

M

T

W

T

f

S

S

>>——▷ priorities ◁——

- _____
- _____
- _____
- _____
- _____
- _____
- _____
- _____
- _____
- _____

my Goals

my motivation

measurements

neck _____
chest _____
biceps _____
waist _____
hips _____
thigh _____
calf _____

weight

weight _____
bmi _____
fat% _____

"You don't have to be extreme, just consistent."

⬗⬗⬗⬗⬗⬗⬗⬗ 😀 🙂 😐 🙁 😣

⬗⬗⬗⬗⬗⬗⬗⬗ 😀 🙂 😐 🙁 😣

⬗⬗⬗⬗⬗⬗⬗⬗ 😀 🙂 😐 🙁 😣

⬗⬗⬗⬗⬗⬗⬗⬗ 😀 🙂 😐 🙁 😣

⬗⬗⬗⬗⬗⬗⬗⬗ 😀 🙂 😐 🙁 😣

⬗⬗⬗⬗⬗⬗⬗⬗ 😀 🙂 😐 🙁 😣

⬗⬗⬗⬗⬗⬗⬗⬗ 😀 🙂 😐 🙁 😣

⪢⟶⟶ Priorities ⟵⟵⪡

- ☐ _____
- ☐ _____
- ☐ _____
- ☐ _____
- ☐ _____
- ☐ _____
- ☐ _____
- ☐ _____
- ☐ _____
- ☐ _____

my goals

my motivation

🦌 measurements 🦌

neck _____
chest _____
biceps _____
waist _____
hips _____
thigh _____
calf _____

🧍 weight 🧍

weight _____
BMI _____
fat% _____

WEEK 24

"The difference between wanting and achieving is discipline."

m

T

W

T

f

S

S

›› → Priorities ←

- _____
- _____
- _____
- _____
- _____
- _____
- _____
- _____
- _____
- _____

--- my Goals ---

--- my motivation

measurements

neck _____
chest _____
Biceps _____
waist _____
Hips _____
Thigh _____
calf _____

weight

weight _____
BMi _____
fat% _____

☐ Track your weight ☐

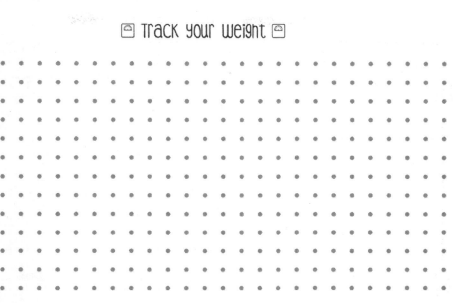

📏 Track your measurements 📏

Date										
y fat %										
neck										
t/chest										
Biceps										
Waist										
Hips										
Thigh										
Calf										

WEEK 25

"Wake up. Work out. Look hot. Kick ass."

m

T

W

T

f

S

S

⇉→⇉ Priorities ⇇←

- _____
- _____
- _____
- _____
- _____
- _____
- _____
- _____
- _____

---- my Goals ----

---- my motivation ----

⊭ measurements ⊭

neck _____
chest _____
Biceps _____
waist _____
Hips _____
Thigh _____
calf _____

🚻 weight 🚻

weight _____
BMI _____
fat% _____

"Go the extra mile. It's never crowded."

⊘⊘⊘⊘⊘⊘⊘⊘⊘ 😃 🙂 😐 🙁 😫

⊘⊘⊘⊘⊘⊘⊘⊘⊘ 😃 🙂 😐 🙁 😫

⊘⊘⊘⊘⊘⊘⊘⊘⊘ 😃 🙂 😐 🙁 😫

⊘⊘⊘⊘⊘⊘⊘⊘⊘ 😃 🙂 😐 🙁 😫

⊘⊘⊘⊘⊘⊘⊘⊘⊘ 😃 🙂 😐 🙁 😫

⊘⊘⊘⊘⊘⊘⊘⊘⊘ 😃 🙂 😐 🙁 😫

⊘⊘⊘⊘⊘⊘⊘⊘⊘ 😃 🙂 😐 🙁 😫

⤞⟶⤇ Priorities ⤆⟵⤝

- ☐ _____
- ☐ _____
- ☐ _____
- ☐ _____
- ☐ _____
- ☐ _____
- ☐ _____
- ☐ _____
- ☐ _____
- ☐ _____

My Goals

My Motivation

🐃 Measurements 🐃

Neck _____
Chest _____
Biceps _____
Waist _____
Hips _____
Thigh _____
Calf _____

🏋 Weight 🏋

Weight _____
BMI _____
Fat% _____

HEALTHY RECIPES

Recipe: _____ Prep Time: _____ Total Time: _____

Rating: ☆ ☆ ☆ ☆ ☆   Difficulty: (E) (M) (D)   Serves: (2) (4) (6)

ingredients

- _____
- _____
- _____
- _____
- _____
- _____
- _____
- _____
- _____
- _____
- _____

Directions

_____
_____
_____
_____
_____
_____
_____
_____
_____
_____
_____
_____
_____
_____
_____
_____

Recipe: _____ Prep Time: _____ Total Time: _____

Rating: ☆ ☆ ☆ ☆ ☆   Difficulty: (E) (M) (D)   Serves: (2) (4) (6)

ingredients

- _____
- _____
- _____
- _____
- _____
- _____
- _____
- _____
- _____
- _____
- _____

Directions

_____
_____
_____
_____
_____
_____
_____
_____
_____
_____
_____
_____
_____
_____
_____
_____

pe: _____ Prep Time: _____ Total Time: _____

ng: ☆ ☆ ☆ ☆ ☆ Difficulty: (E) (M) (D) Serves: (2) (4) (6) (8)

ingredients

Directions

_____

---

pe: _____ Prep Time: _____ Total Time: _____

ng: ☆ ☆ ☆ ☆ ☆ Difficulty: (E) (M) (D) Serves: (2) (4) (6) (8)

ngredients

Directions

HEALTHY RECIPES

Recipe: _____ Prep Time: _____ Total Time: _____

Rating: ☆ ☆ ☆ ☆ ☆   Difficulty: (E) (M) (D)   Serves: (2) (4) (6)

ingredients
- ○ _____
- ○ _____
- ○ _____
- ○ _____
- ○ _____
- ○ _____
- ○ _____
- ○ _____
- ○ _____
- ○ _____
- ○ _____
- ○ _____

Directions
_____
_____
_____
_____
_____
_____
_____
_____
_____
_____
_____
_____
_____
_____
_____
_____

Recipe: _____ Prep Time: _____ Total Time: _____

Rating: ☆ ☆ ☆ ☆ ☆   Difficulty: (E) (M) (D)   Serves: (2) (4) (6)

ingredients
- ○ _____
- ○ _____
- ○ _____
- ○ _____
- ○ _____
- ○ _____
- ○ _____
- ○ _____
- ○ _____
- ○ _____
- ○ _____
- ○ _____

Directions
_____
_____
_____
_____
_____
_____
_____
_____
_____
_____
_____
_____
_____
_____
_____
_____

HEALTHY RECIPES

Pe: _____ Prep Time: _____ Total Time: _____

ng: ☆ ☆ ☆ ☆ ☆   Difficulty: Ⓔ Ⓜ Ⓓ   Serves: ② ④ ⑥ ⑧

⌐ Ingredients ─────   ⌐ Directions ──────────

_____   _____
_____   _____
_____   _____
_____   _____
_____   _____
_____   _____
_____   _____
_____   _____
_____   _____
_____   _____
_____   _____
_____   _____
_____   _____
_____   _____
                         _____

Pe: _____ Prep Time: _____ Total Time: _____

ng: ☆ ☆ ☆ ☆ ☆   Difficulty: Ⓔ Ⓜ Ⓓ   Serves: ② ④ ⑥ ⑧

⌐ Ingredients ─────   ⌐ Directions ──────────

_____   _____
_____   _____
_____   _____
_____   _____
_____   _____
_____   _____
_____   _____
_____   _____
_____   _____
_____   _____
_____   _____
_____   _____
_____   _____
                         _____

HEALTHY RECIPES

Recipe: _____ Prep Time: _____ Total Time: _____

Rating: ☆ ☆ ☆ ☆ ☆   Difficulty: Ⓔ Ⓜ Ⓓ   Serves: ② ④ ⑥

ingredients

- ☐ _____
- ☐ _____
- ☐ _____
- ☐ _____
- ☐ _____
- ☐ _____
- ☐ _____
- ☐ _____
- ☐ _____
- ☐ _____
- ☐ _____
- ☐ _____

Directions

_____
_____
_____
_____
_____
_____
_____
_____
_____
_____
_____
_____
_____
_____
_____

Recipe: _____ Prep Time: _____ Total Time: _____

Rating: ☆ ☆ ☆ ☆ ☆   Difficulty: Ⓔ Ⓜ Ⓓ   Serves: ② ④ ⑥

ingredients

- ☐ _____
- ☐ _____
- ☐ _____
- ☐ _____
- ☐ _____
- ☐ _____
- ☐ _____
- ☐ _____
- ☐ _____
- ☐ _____
- ☐ _____
- ☐ _____

Directions

_____
_____
_____
_____
_____
_____
_____
_____
_____
_____
_____
_____
_____
_____
_____

HEALTHY RECIPES

pe: _____ Prep Time: _____ Total Time: _____

ng: ☆ ☆ ☆ ☆ ☆   Difficulty: Ⓔ Ⓜ Ⓓ   Serves: ② ④ ⑥ ⑧

Ingredients ————   Directions ————

pe: _____ Prep Time: _____ Total Time: _____

ng: ☆ ☆ ☆ ☆ ☆   Difficulty: Ⓔ Ⓜ Ⓓ   Serves: ② ④ ⑥ ⑧

Ingredients ————   Directions ————

HEALTHY RECIPES

Recipe: _____ Prep Time: _____ Total Time: _____

Rating: ☆ ☆ ☆ ☆ ☆   Difficulty: (E) (M) (D)   Serves: (2) (4) (6)

ingredients

- ◌ _____
- ◌ _____
- ◌ _____
- ◌ _____
- ◌ _____
- ◌ _____
- ◌ _____
- ◌ _____
- ◌ _____
- ◌ _____
- ◌ _____
- ◌ _____

Directions

_____
_____
_____
_____
_____
_____
_____
_____
_____
_____
_____
_____
_____
_____
_____

Recipe: _____ Prep Time: _____ Total Time: _____

Rating: ☆ ☆ ☆ ☆ ☆   Difficulty: (E) (M) (D)   Serves: (2) (4) (6)

ingredients

- ◌ _____
- ◌ _____
- ◌ _____
- ◌ _____
- ◌ _____
- ◌ _____
- ◌ _____
- ◌ _____
- ◌ _____
- ◌ _____
- ◌ _____
- ◌ _____

Directions

_____
_____
_____
_____
_____
_____
_____
_____
_____
_____
_____
_____
_____
_____
_____

HEALTHY RECIPES

Recipe: _____ **Prep Time:** _____ **Total Time:** _____

Rating: ☆ ☆ ☆ ☆ ☆ **Difficulty:** (E) (M) (D) **Serves:** (2) (4) (6) (8)

Ingredients
- _____
- _____
- _____
- _____
- _____
- _____
- _____
- _____
- _____
- _____
- _____

Directions
_____
_____
_____
_____
_____
_____
_____
_____
_____
_____
_____
_____
_____
_____
_____

Recipe: _____ **Prep Time:** _____ **Total Time:** _____

Rating: ☆ ☆ ☆ ☆ ☆ **Difficulty:** (E) (M) (D) **Serves:** (2) (4) (6) (8)

Ingredients
- _____
- _____
- _____
- _____
- _____
- _____
- _____
- _____
- _____
- _____
- _____

Directions
_____
_____
_____
_____
_____
_____
_____
_____
_____
_____
_____
_____
_____
_____
_____

HEALTHY RECIPES

Recipe: _____ Prep Time: _____ Total Time: ____

Rating: ☆ ☆ ☆ ☆ ☆   Difficulty: (E) (M) (D)   Serves: (2) (4) (

Ingredients

- ○ _____
- ○ _____
- ○ _____
- ○ _____
- ○ _____
- ○ _____
- ○ _____
- ○ _____
- ○ _____
- ○ _____
- ○ _____
- ○ _____

Directions

_____
_____
_____
_____
_____
_____
_____
_____
_____
_____
_____
_____
_____
_____

Recipe: _____ Prep Time: _____ Total Time: ____

Rating: ☆ ☆ ☆ ☆ ☆   Difficulty: (E) (M) (D)   Serves: (2) (4) (

Ingredients

- ○ _____
- ○ _____
- ○ _____
- ○ _____
- ○ _____
- ○ _____
- ○ _____
- ○ _____
- ○ _____
- ○ _____
- ○ _____
- ○ _____

Directions

_____
_____
_____
_____
_____
_____
_____
_____
_____
_____
_____
_____
_____
_____

pe: _____ Prep Time: _____ Total Time: _____

ng: ☆ ☆ ☆ ☆ ☆ Difficulty: (E) (M) (D) Serves: (2) (4) (6) (8)

Ingredients ―――――

_____
_____
_____
_____
_____
_____
_____
_____
_____
_____

Directions ―――――

_____
_____
_____
_____
_____
_____
_____
_____
_____
_____
_____
_____
_____
_____
_____

pe: _____ Prep Time: _____ Total Time: _____

ng: ☆ ☆ ☆ ☆ ☆ Difficulty: (E) (M) (D) Serves: (2) (4) (6) (8)

Ingredients ―――――

_____
_____
_____
_____
_____
_____
_____
_____
_____

Directions ―――――

_____
_____
_____
_____
_____
_____
_____
_____
_____
_____
_____
_____
_____

GROCERY LIST

Fresh Produce

- [ ] _____
- [ ] _____
- [ ] _____
- [ ] _____
- [ ] _____
- [ ] _____
- [ ] _____
- [ ] _____
- [ ] _____
- [ ] _____

Protein/Meat

- [ ] _____
- [ ] _____
- [ ] _____
- [ ] _____
- [ ] _____
- [ ] _____
- [ ] _____
- [ ] _____
- [ ] _____
- [ ] _____

Grains/Brea

- [ ] _____
- [ ] _____
- [ ] _____
- [ ] _____
- [ ] _____
- [ ] _____
- [ ] _____
- [ ] _____
- [ ] _____
- [ ] _____

Frozen Foods

- [ ] _____
- [ ] _____
- [ ] _____
- [ ] _____
- [ ] _____
- [ ] _____
- [ ] _____
- [ ] _____
- [ ] _____
- [ ] _____

Cans/Packages

- [ ] _____
- [ ] _____
- [ ] _____
- [ ] _____
- [ ] _____
- [ ] _____
- [ ] _____
- [ ] _____
- [ ] _____

Others/Mis

- [ ] _____
- [ ] _____
- [ ] _____
- [ ] _____
- [ ] _____
- [ ] _____
- [ ] _____
- [ ] _____
- [ ] _____
- [ ] _____
- [ ] _____
- [ ] _____
- [ ] _____
- [ ] _____
- [ ] _____
- [ ] _____
- [ ] _____
- [ ] _____

Dairy Products

- [ ] _____
- [ ] _____
- [ ] _____
- [ ] _____
- [ ] _____
- [ ] _____
- [ ] _____
- [ ] _____
- [ ] _____
- [ ] _____

Household Items

- [ ] _____
- [ ] _____
- [ ] _____
- [ ] _____
- [ ] _____
- [ ] _____
- [ ] _____
- [ ] _____
- [ ] _____
- [ ] _____

GROCERY LIST

Fresh Produce

_____
_____
_____
_____
_____
_____
_____
_____
_____
_____

Protein/Meat

- _____
- _____
- _____
- _____
- _____
- _____
- _____
- _____
- _____
- _____

Grains/Bread

- _____
- _____
- _____
- _____
- _____
- _____
- _____
- _____
- _____
- _____

Frozen Foods

_____
_____
_____
_____
_____
_____
_____
_____
_____

Cans/Packages

- _____
- _____
- _____
- _____
- _____
- _____
- _____
- _____
- _____

Others/Misc

- _____
- _____
- _____
- _____
- _____
- _____
- _____
- _____
- _____
- _____
- _____
- _____
- _____
- _____
- _____
- _____
- _____
- _____
- _____

Dairy Products

_____
_____
_____
_____
_____
_____
_____
_____
_____

Household Items

- _____
- _____
- _____
- _____
- _____
- _____
- _____
- _____
- _____
- _____

GROCERY LIST

🥬 Fresh Produce

- ○ _____
- ○ _____
- ○ _____
- ○ _____
- ○ _____
- ○ _____
- ○ _____
- ○ _____
- ○ _____
- ○ _____

🐟 Protein/Meat

- ○ _____
- ○ _____
- ○ _____
- ○ _____
- ○ _____
- ○ _____
- ○ _____
- ○ _____
- ○ _____
- ○ _____

🍞 Grains/Bread

- ○ _____
- ○ _____
- ○ _____
- ○ _____
- ○ _____
- ○ _____
- ○ _____
- ○ _____
- ○ _____

🍦 Frozen Foods

- ○ _____
- ○ _____
- ○ _____
- ○ _____
- ○ _____
- ○ _____
- ○ _____
- ○ _____
- ○ _____
- ○ _____

🥫 Cans/Packages

- ○ _____
- ○ _____
- ○ _____
- ○ _____
- ○ _____
- ○ _____
- ○ _____
- ○ _____
- ○ _____

🖼 Others/Misc

- ○ _____
- ○ _____
- ○ _____
- ○ _____
- ○ _____
- ○ _____
- ○ _____
- ○ _____
- ○ _____
- ○ _____
- ○ _____
- ○ _____
- ○ _____
- ○ _____

🥛 Dairy Products

- ○ _____
- ○ _____
- ○ _____
- ○ _____
- ○ _____
- ○ _____
- ○ _____
- ○ _____
- ○ _____
- ○ _____

🧴 Household Items

- ○ _____
- ○ _____
- ○ _____
- ○ _____
- ○ _____
- ○ _____
- ○ _____
- ○ _____
- ○ _____

GROCERY LIST

fresh produce

Protein/meat

Grains/Bread

frozen foods

cans/packages

others/misc

Dairy Products

Household items

GROCERY LIST

🍓 Fresh Produce

- ⬚ _____
- ⬚ _____
- ⬚ _____
- ⬚ _____
- ⬚ _____
- ⬚ _____
- ⬚ _____
- ⬚ _____
- ⬚ _____
- ⬚ _____

🐟 Protein/Meat

- ⬚ _____
- ⬚ _____
- ⬚ _____
- ⬚ _____
- ⬚ _____
- ⬚ _____
- ⬚ _____
- ⬚ _____
- ⬚ _____
- ⬚ _____

🍞 Grains/Bread

- ⬚ _____
- ⬚ _____
- ⬚ _____
- ⬚ _____
- ⬚ _____
- ⬚ _____
- ⬚ _____
- ⬚ _____
- ⬚ _____

🍦 Frozen Foods

- ⬚ _____
- ⬚ _____
- ⬚ _____
- ⬚ _____
- ⬚ _____
- ⬚ _____
- ⬚ _____
- ⬚ _____
- ⬚ _____
- ⬚ _____

🥫 Cans/Packages

- ⬚ _____
- ⬚ _____
- ⬚ _____
- ⬚ _____
- ⬚ _____
- ⬚ _____
- ⬚ _____
- ⬚ _____
- ⬚ _____
- ⬚ _____

🛒 Others/Misc

- ⬚ _____
- ⬚ _____
- ⬚ _____
- ⬚ _____
- ⬚ _____
- ⬚ _____
- ⬚ _____
- ⬚ _____
- ⬚ _____
- ⬚ _____
- ⬚ _____
- ⬚ _____
- ⬚ _____
- ⬚ _____
- ⬚ _____
- ⬚ _____

🥛 Dairy Products

- ⬚ _____
- ⬚ _____
- ⬚ _____
- ⬚ _____
- ⬚ _____
- ⬚ _____
- ⬚ _____
- ⬚ _____
- ⬚ _____
- ⬚ _____

🧴 Household Items

- ⬚ _____
- ⬚ _____
- ⬚ _____
- ⬚ _____
- ⬚ _____
- ⬚ _____
- ⬚ _____
- ⬚ _____
- ⬚ _____
- ⬚ _____

GROCERY LIST

fresh produce

- _____
- _____
- _____
- _____
- _____
- _____
- _____
- _____
- _____
- _____

protein/meat

- _____
- _____
- _____
- _____
- _____
- _____
- _____
- _____
- _____
- _____

Grains/Bread

- _____
- _____
- _____
- _____
- _____
- _____
- _____
- _____
- _____

frozen foods

- _____
- _____
- _____
- _____
- _____
- _____
- _____
- _____

cans/packages

- _____
- _____
- _____
- _____
- _____
- _____
- _____
- _____
- _____

others/misc

- _____
- _____
- _____
- _____
- _____
- _____
- _____
- _____
- _____
- _____
- _____
- _____
- _____

dairy products

- _____
- _____
- _____
- _____
- _____
- _____
- _____
- _____

Household items

- _____
- _____
- _____
- _____
- _____
- _____
- _____
- _____
- _____

GROCERY LIST

fresh produce

- _____
- _____
- _____
- _____
- _____
- _____
- _____
- _____
- _____
- _____

protein/meat

- _____
- _____
- _____
- _____
- _____
- _____
- _____
- _____
- _____
- _____

Grains/Bread

- _____
- _____
- _____
- _____
- _____
- _____
- _____
- _____
- _____
- _____

frozen foods

- _____
- _____
- _____
- _____
- _____
- _____
- _____
- _____
- _____
- _____

cans/packages

- _____
- _____
- _____
- _____
- _____
- _____
- _____
- _____
- _____
- _____

others/misc

- _____
- _____
- _____
- _____
- _____
- _____
- _____
- _____
- _____
- _____
- _____
- _____
- _____
- _____

Dairy Products

- _____
- _____
- _____
- _____
- _____
- _____
- _____
- _____
- _____
- _____

Household items

- _____
- _____
- _____
- _____
- _____
- _____
- _____
- _____
- _____
- _____

GROCERY LIST

Fresh Produce

_____
_____
_____
_____
_____
_____
_____
_____
_____
_____

Protein/Meat

○ _____
○ _____
○ _____
○ _____
○ _____
○ _____
○ _____
○ _____
○ _____
○ _____

Grains/Bread

○ _____
○ _____
○ _____
○ _____
○ _____
○ _____
○ _____
○ _____
○ _____
○ _____

Frozen Foods

_____
_____
_____
_____
_____
_____
_____
_____

Cans/Packages

○ _____
○ _____
○ _____
○ _____
○ _____
○ _____
○ _____
○ _____
○ _____
○ _____

Others/Misc

○ _____
○ _____
○ _____
○ _____
○ _____
○ _____
○ _____
○ _____
○ _____
○ _____
○ _____
○ _____
○ _____
○ _____
○ _____
○ _____

Dairy Products

_____
_____
_____
_____
_____
_____
_____
_____

Household Items

○ _____
○ _____
○ _____
○ _____
○ _____
○ _____
○ _____
○ _____
○ _____
○ _____

GROCERY LIST

fresh Produce

- ○ _____
- ○ _____
- ○ _____
- ○ _____
- ○ _____
- ○ _____
- ○ _____
- ○ _____
- ○ _____
- ○ _____

Protein/meat

- ○ _____
- ○ _____
- ○ _____
- ○ _____
- ○ _____
- ○ _____
- ○ _____
- ○ _____
- ○ _____
- ○ _____

Grains/Brea

- ○ _____
- ○ _____
- ○ _____
- ○ _____
- ○ _____
- ○ _____
- ○ _____
- ○ _____
- ○ _____
- ○ _____

frozen foods

- ○ _____
- ○ _____
- ○ _____
- ○ _____
- ○ _____
- ○ _____
- ○ _____
- ○ _____
- ○ _____
- ○ _____

cans/Packages

- ○ _____
- ○ _____
- ○ _____
- ○ _____
- ○ _____
- ○ _____
- ○ _____
- ○ _____
- ○ _____

others/misc

- ○ _____
- ○ _____
- ○ _____
- ○ _____
- ○ _____
- ○ _____
- ○ _____
- ○ _____
- ○ _____
- ○ _____
- ○ _____
- ○ _____
- ○ _____
- ○ _____

Dairy Products

- ○ _____
- ○ _____
- ○ _____
- ○ _____
- ○ _____
- ○ _____
- ○ _____
- ○ _____
- ○ _____
- ○ _____

Household items

- ○ _____
- ○ _____
- ○ _____
- ○ _____
- ○ _____
- ○ _____
- ○ _____
- ○ _____
- ○ _____
- ○ _____

GROCERY LIST

Fresh Produce

- _____
- _____
- _____
- _____
- _____
- _____
- _____
- _____

Protein/Meat

- _____
- _____
- _____
- _____
- _____
- _____
- _____
- _____
- _____
- _____

Grains/Bread

- _____
- _____
- _____
- _____
- _____
- _____
- _____
- _____

Frozen Foods

- _____
- _____
- _____
- _____
- _____
- _____
- _____

Cans/Packages

- _____
- _____
- _____
- _____
- _____
- _____
- _____
- _____

Others/Misc

- _____
- _____
- _____
- _____
- _____
- _____
- _____
- _____
- _____
- _____
- _____
- _____
- _____

Dairy Products

- _____
- _____
- _____
- _____
- _____

Household Items

- _____
- _____
- _____
- _____
- _____
- _____
- _____
- _____
- _____

MEDICATION TRACKER

medication/supplement: _____ month: _____

notes:

(1) (2) (3) (4) (5) (6) (7) (8) (9) (1

(12) (13) (14) (15) (16) (17) (18) (19) (20) (21

(23) (24) (25) (26) (27) (28) (29) (30) (31)

medication/supplement: _____ month: _____

(1) (2) (3) (4) (5) (6) (7) (8) (9) (10) (11)

(12) (13) (14) (15) (16) (17) (18) (19) (20) (21) (22)

(23) (24) (25) (26) (27) (28) (29) (30) (31)

notes:

medication/supplement: _____ month: _____

notes:

(1) (2) (3) (4) (5) (6) (7) (8) (9) (1(

(12) (13) (14) (15) (16) (17) (18) (19) (20) (21

(23) (24) (25) (26) (27) (28) (29) (30) (31)

medication/supplement: _____ month: _____

(1) (2) (3) (4) (5) (6) (7) (8) (9) (10) (11)

(12) (13) (14) (15) (16) (17) (18) (19) (20) (21) (22)

(23) (24) (25) (26) (27) (28) (29) (30) (31)

notes:

MEDICATION TRACKER

cation/supplement: _____ month: _____

notes: ─────────

①②③④⑤⑥⑦⑧⑨⑩⑪

⑫⑬⑭⑮⑯⑰⑱⑲⑳㉑㉒

㉓㉔㉕㉖㉗㉘㉙㉚㉛

cation/supplement: _____ month: _____

②③④⑤⑥⑦⑧⑨⑩⑪

⑬⑭⑮⑯⑰⑱⑲⑳㉑㉒

㉔㉕㉖㉗㉘㉙㉚㉛

notes: ─────────

cation/supplement: _____ month: _____

notes: ─────────

①②③④⑤⑥⑦⑧⑨⑩⑪

⑫⑬⑭⑮⑯⑰⑱⑲⑳㉑㉒

㉓㉔㉕㉖㉗㉘㉙㉚㉛

cation/supplement: _____ month: _____

②③④⑤⑥⑦⑧⑨⑩⑪

⑬⑭⑮⑯⑰⑱⑲⑳㉑㉒

㉔㉕㉖㉗㉘㉙㉚㉛

notes: ─────────

MEDICATION TRACKER

medication/supplement: _____ month: _____

notes: _____

① ② ③ ④ ⑤ ⑥ ⑦ ⑧ ⑨ ⑩
⑫ ⑬ ⑭ ⑮ ⑯ ⑰ ⑱ ⑲ ⑳ ㉑
㉓ ㉔ ㉕ ㉖ ㉗ ㉘ ㉙ ㉚ ㉛

medication/supplement: _____ month: _____

① ② ③ ④ ⑤ ⑥ ⑦ ⑧ ⑨ ⑩ ⑪
⑫ ⑬ ⑭ ⑮ ⑯ ⑰ ⑱ ⑲ ⑳ ㉑ ㉒
㉓ ㉔ ㉕ ㉖ ㉗ ㉘ ㉙ ㉚ ㉛

notes: _____

medication/supplement: _____ month: _____

notes: _____

① ② ③ ④ ⑤ ⑥ ⑦ ⑧ ⑨ ⑩
⑫ ⑬ ⑭ ⑮ ⑯ ⑰ ⑱ ⑲ ⑳ ㉑
㉓ ㉔ ㉕ ㉖ ㉗ ㉘ ㉙ ㉚ ㉛

medication/supplement: _____ month: _____

① ② ③ ④ ⑤ ⑥ ⑦ ⑧ ⑨ ⑩ ⑪
⑫ ⑬ ⑭ ⑮ ⑯ ⑰ ⑱ ⑲ ⑳ ㉑ ㉒
㉓ ㉔ ㉕ ㉖ ㉗ ㉘ ㉙ ㉚ ㉛

notes: _____

MEDICATION TRACKER

cation/supplement: _____ month: _____

notes: _____

```
(1) (2) (3) (4) (5) (6) (7) (8) (9) (10) (11)
(12) (13) (14) (15) (16) (17) (18) (19) (20) (21) (22)
(23) (24) (25) (26) (27) (28) (29) (30) (31)
```

cation/supplement: _____ month: _____

```
(2) (3) (4) (5) (6) (7) (8) (9) (10) (11)
(13) (14) (15) (16) (17) (18) (19) (20) (21) (22)
(24) (25) (26) (27) (28) (29) (30) (31)
```

notes: _____

cation/supplement: _____ month: _____

notes: _____

```
(1) (2) (3) (4) (5) (6) (7) (8) (9) (10) (11)
(12) (13) (14) (15) (16) (17) (18) (19) (20) (21) (22)
(23) (24) (25) (26) (27) (28) (29) (30) (31)
```

cation/supplement: _____ month: _____

```
(2) (3) (4) (5) (6) (7) (8) (9) (10) (11)
(13) (14) (15) (16) (17) (18) (19) (20) (21) (22)
(24) (25) (26) (27) (28) (29) (30) (31)
```

notes: _____

MEDICATION TRACKER

medication/supplement: _____ month: _____

notes:

(1) (2) (3) (4) (5) (6) (7) (8) (9) (10)

(12) (13) (14) (15) (16) (17) (18) (19) (20) (21)

(23) (24) (25) (26) (27) (28) (29) (30) (31)

medication/supplement: _____ month: _____

(1) (2) (3) (4) (5) (6) (7) (8) (9) (10) (11)

(12) (13) (14) (15) (16) (17) (18) (19) (20) (21) (22)

(23) (24) (25) (26) (27) (28) (29) (30) (31)

notes:

medication/supplement: _____ month: _____

notes:

(1) (2) (3) (4) (5) (6) (7) (8) (9) (10)

(12) (13) (14) (15) (16) (17) (18) (19) (20) (21)

(23) (24) (25) (26) (27) (28) (29) (30) (31)

medication/supplement: _____ month: _____

(1) (2) (3) (4) (5) (6) (7) (8) (9) (10) (11)

(12) (13) (14) (15) (16) (17) (18) (19) (20) (21) (22)

(23) (24) (25) (26) (27) (28) (29) (30) (31)

notes:

MEDICATION TRACKER

MEDICATION TRACKER

medication/supplement: _____ month: _____

notes:

(1) (2) (3) (4) (5) (6) (7) (8) (9) (10) (11)
(12) (13) (14) (15) (16) (17) (18) (19) (20) (21) (22)
(23) (24) (25) (26) (27) (28) (29) (30) (31)

medication/supplement: _____ month: _____

(2) (3) (4) (5) (6) (7) (8) (9) (10) (11)
(13) (14) (15) (16) (17) (18) (19) (20) (21) (22)
(24) (25) (26) (27) (28) (29) (30) (31)

notes:

medication/supplement: _____ month: _____

notes:

(1) (2) (3) (4) (5) (6) (7) (8) (9) (10) (11)
(12) (13) (14) (15) (16) (17) (18) (19) (20) (21) (22)
(23) (24) (25) (26) (27) (28) (29) (30) (31)

medication/supplement: _____ month: _____

(2) (3) (4) (5) (6) (7) (8) (9) (10) (11)
(13) (14) (15) (16) (17) (18) (19) (20) (21) (22)
(24) (25) (26) (27) (28) (29) (30) (31)

notes:

MEDICATION TRACKER

medication/supplement: _____ month: _____

┌─ notes: ─────────────────────┐
│   │
│   │
│   │
│   │
└──────────────────────────────┘

① ② ③ ④ ⑤ ⑥ ⑦ ⑧ ⑨ ⑩
⑫ ⑬ ⑭ ⑮ ⑯ ⑰ ⑱ ⑲ ⑳ ㉑
㉓ ㉔ ㉕ ㉖ ㉗ ㉘ ㉙ ㉚ ㉛

medication/supplement: _____ month: _____

① ② ③ ④ ⑤ ⑥ ⑦ ⑧ ⑨ ⑩ ⑪
⑫ ⑬ ⑭ ⑮ ⑯ ⑰ ⑱ ⑲ ⑳ ㉑ ㉒
㉓ ㉔ ㉕ ㉖ ㉗ ㉘ ㉙ ㉚ ㉛

┌─ notes: ─────────────────────┐
│   │
│   │
│   │
│   │
└──────────────────────────────┘

medication/supplement: _____ month: _____

┌─ notes: ─────────────────────┐
│   │
│   │
│   │
│   │
└──────────────────────────────┘

① ② ③ ④ ⑤ ⑥ ⑦ ⑧ ⑨ ⑩
⑫ ⑬ ⑭ ⑮ ⑯ ⑰ ⑱ ⑲ ⑳ ㉑
㉓ ㉔ ㉕ ㉖ ㉗ ㉘ ㉙ ㉚ ㉛

medication/supplement: _____ month: _____

① ② ③ ④ ⑤ ⑥ ⑦ ⑧ ⑨ ⑩ ⑪
⑫ ⑬ ⑭ ⑮ ⑯ ⑰ ⑱ ⑲ ⑳ ㉑ ㉒
㉓ ㉔ ㉕ ㉖ ㉗ ㉘ ㉙ ㉚ ㉛

┌─ notes: ─────────────────────┐
│   │
│   │
│   │
│   │
└──────────────────────────────┘

MEDICATION TRACKER

cation/supplement: _____ month: _____

notes: ─────────────

(1) (2) (3) (4) (5) (6) (7) (8) (9) (10) (11)

(12) (13) (14) (15) (16) (17) (18) (19) (20) (21) (22)

(23) (24) (25) (26) (27) (28) (29) (30) (31)

cation/supplement: _____ month: _____

(2) (3) (4) (5) (6) (7) (8) (9) (10) (11)

(3) (14) (15) (16) (17) (18) (19) (20) (21) (22)

(4) (25) (26) (27) (28) (29) (30) (31)

notes: ─────────────

cation/supplement: _____ month: _____

notes: ─────────────

(1) (2) (3) (4) (5) (6) (7) (8) (9) (10) (11)

(12) (13) (14) (15) (16) (17) (18) (19) (20) (21) (22)

(23) (24) (25) (26) (27) (28) (29) (30) (31)

cation/supplement: _____ month: _____

(2) (3) (4) (5) (6) (7) (8) (9) (10) (11)

(3) (14) (15) (16) (17) (18) (19) (20) (21) (22)

(4) (25) (26) (27) (28) (29) (30) (31)

notes: ─────────────

MEDICATION TRACKER

medication/supplement: _____ month: _____

notes: _____
┌─────────────────────────┐
│   │
│   │
│   │
│   │
└─────────────────────────┘

① ② ③ ④ ⑤ ⑥ ⑦ ⑧ ⑨ ⑩
⑫ ⑬ ⑭ ⑮ ⑯ ⑰ ⑱ ⑲ ⑳ ㉑
㉓ ㉔ ㉕ ㉖ ㉗ ㉘ ㉙ ㉚ ㉛

medication/supplement: _____ month: _____

① ② ③ ④ ⑤ ⑥ ⑦ ⑧ ⑨ ⑩ ⑪
⑫ ⑬ ⑭ ⑮ ⑯ ⑰ ⑱ ⑲ ⑳ ㉑ ㉒
㉓ ㉔ ㉕ ㉖ ㉗ ㉘ ㉙ ㉚ ㉛

notes: _____
┌─────────────────────────┐
│   │
│   │
│   │
└─────────────────────────┘

medication/supplement: _____ month: _____

notes: _____
┌─────────────────────────┐
│   │
│   │
│   │
│   │
└─────────────────────────┘

① ② ③ ④ ⑤ ⑥ ⑦ ⑧ ⑨ ⑩
⑫ ⑬ ⑭ ⑮ ⑯ ⑰ ⑱ ⑲ ⑳ ㉑
㉓ ㉔ ㉕ ㉖ ㉗ ㉘ ㉙ ㉚ ㉛

medication/supplement: _____ month: _____

① ② ③ ④ ⑤ ⑥ ⑦ ⑧ ⑨ ⑩ ⑪
⑫ ⑬ ⑭ ⑮ ⑯ ⑰ ⑱ ⑲ ⑳ ㉑ ㉒
㉓ ㉔ ㉕ ㉖ ㉗ ㉘ ㉙ ㉚ ㉛

notes: _____
┌─────────────────────────┐
│   │
│   │
│   │
└─────────────────────────┘

MEDICATION TRACKER

ication/supplement: _____ month: _____

notes: _____

1 2 3 4 5 6 7 8 9 10 11
12 13 14 15 16 17 18 19 20 21 22
23 24 25 26 27 28 29 30 31

ication/supplement: _____ month: _____

2 3 4 5 6 7 8 9 10 11
13 14 15 16 17 18 19 20 21 22
24 25 26 27 28 29 30 31

notes: _____

cation/supplement: _____ month: _____

notes: _____

1 2 3 4 5 6 7 8 9 10 11
12 13 14 15 16 17 18 19 20 21 22
23 24 25 26 27 28 29 30 31

cation/supplement: _____ month: _____

2 3 4 5 6 7 8 9 10 11
13 14 15 16 17 18 19 20 21 22
24 25 26 27 28 29 30 31

notes: _____

HABIT TRACKER

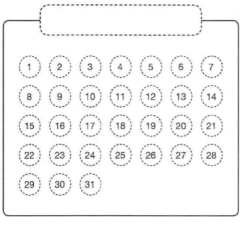

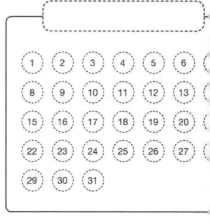

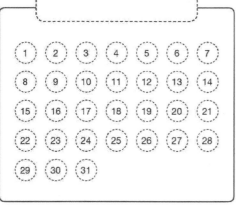

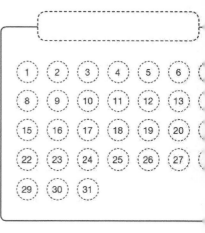

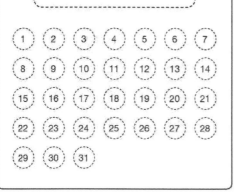

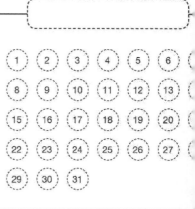

HABIT TRACKER

87

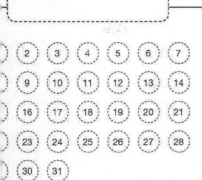

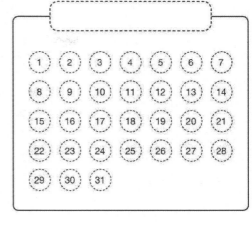

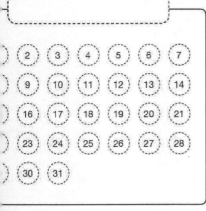

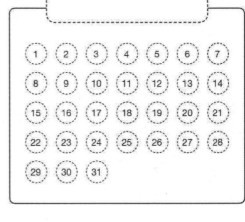

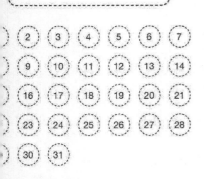

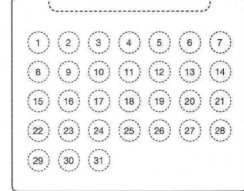

HABIT TRACKER

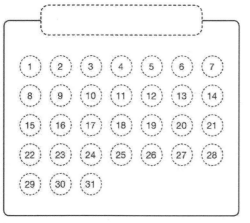

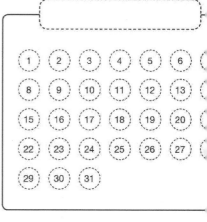

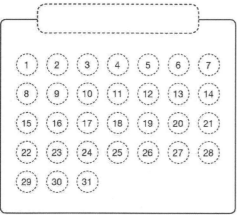

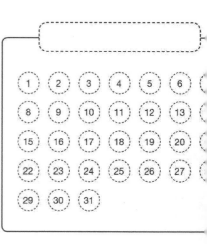

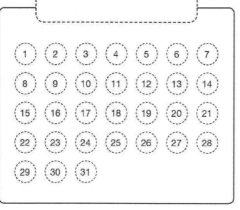

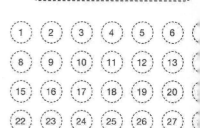

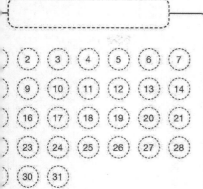

	2	3	4	5	6	7
9	10	11	12	13	14
16	17	18	19	20	21
23	24	25	26	27	28
30	31

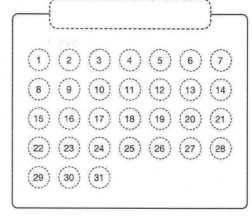

1	2	3	4	5	6	7
8	9	10	11	12	13	14
15	16	17	18	19	20	21
22	23	24	25	26	27	28
29	30	31

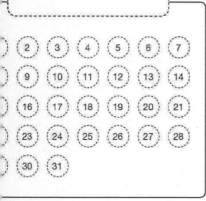

	2	3	4	5	6	7
9	10	11	12	13	14
16	17	18	19	20	21
23	24	25	26	27	28
30	31

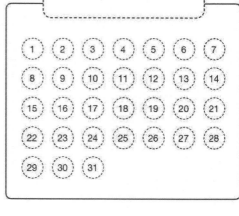

1	2	3	4	5	6	7
8	9	10	11	12	13	14
15	16	17	18	19	20	21
22	23	24	25	26	27	28
29	30	31

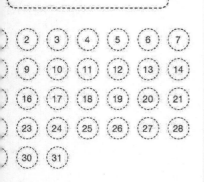

	2	3	4	5	6	7
9	10	11	12	13	14
16	17	18	19	20	21
23	24	25	26	27	28
30	31

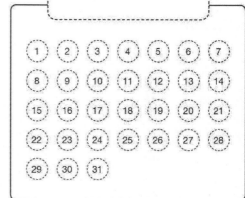

1	2	3	4	5	6	7
8	9	10	11	12	13	14
15	16	17	18	19	20	21
22	23	24	25	26	27	28
29	30	31

HABIT TRACKER

1	2	3	4	5	6	7
8	9	10	11	12	13	14
15	16	17	18	19	20	21
22	23	24	25	26	27	28
29	30	31				

1	2	3	4	5	6	7
8	9	10	11	12	13	14
15	16	17	18	19	20	21
22	23	24	25	26	27	28
29	30	31				

1	2	3	4	5	6	7
8	9	10	11	12	13	14
15	16	17	18	19	20	21
22	23	24	25	26	27	28
29	30	31				

1	2	3	4	5	6	7
8	9	10	11	12	13	14
15	16	17	18	19	20	21
22	23	24	25	26	27	28
29	30	31				

1	2	3	4	5	6	7
8	9	10	11	12	13	14
15	16	17	18	19	20	21
22	23	24	25	26	27	28
29	30	31				

1	2	3	4	5	6	7
8	9	10	11	12	13	14
15	16	17	18	19	20	21
22	23	24	25	26	27	28
29	30	31				

NOTES:

Made in the USA
Monee, IL
06 April 2022

94205500R00061